Key Stage
Spelling

Name ________________________________

Practice sentences

What a lovely surprise! What ___________ they would have! John stood and ___________ at the poster ___________ excitement. The ___________ was coming to town. He rushed around to tell all his friends the ___________ news.

GINN

Test I Camping Capers

"That spot looks __________ for camping," shouted Jane, pointing to a clearing in the __________. "Great," __________ Paul, "but let's camp closer to the stream, it'll be handy for washing up and __________ our clothes." Paul was always looking for the easy __________.

Having __________ the tent they searched through the __________ to find the camping stove and set about cooking their first meal under the stars. It tasted __________.

"What a life!" sighed Paul. "Away from the hustle and bustle of the city with nothing but blue __________, trees and green, green grass as far as the eye can see."

"Don't forget the cows __________ in the field," said Jane. They sat talking for ages before __________ climbing into their sleeping bags and __________ down for the night.

Just as dawn broke they were ____________ awoken by the sound of ____________. "What's going on?" asked Paul ____________.

Before Jane could answer a loud mooing noise was heard and then a cow's head ____________ through the tent flaps.

"We're surrounded by cows!" exclaimed Paul. He ____________ in ____________ as the herd marched past the tent and began to drink from the stream. "Oh no, that stream must be their ____________ drinking place!" he groaned.

"So much for the countryside being ____________," teased Jane.

Test 2 Lost!

The journey up the mountain road was exciting as the car wound its ___________ around hairpin bends with ___________ rocky cliffs on either ___________. Amtiaz and Shirin looked out of the window breathlessly as the car ___________ slowly upwards with its ___________ straining.

Soon their father turned off the main road on to a narrow mountain track, leading into a wooded ___________, filled with pine trees. They found a clearing near a stream, where the water gurgled and bubbled happily along. It was a ___________ place to stop. Amtiaz and Shirin jumped ___________ out of the car and raced to ___________ the area whilst their parents were busy laying out a blanket on the ground and getting out the picnic things.

The children threw rocks into the stream to make ___________ stones. Amtiaz roared with ___________ as Shirin slipped and ___________ into the water as they crossed to the other side. The adults were still preparing the picnic so the children ____________ to follow the narrow path into the forest.

Deeper and deeper it took them until they were ____________ in the ____________ of the forest and could no longer hear the ____________ of their parents. ____________ it was getting a little creepy, the children dared each other to continue until the path seemed to ____________ altogether. As they looked back ____________ looked different. ____________ they realized they were lost.

Test 3 Gorillas and Gibbons

It is hard to believe that gorillas are really ___________, gentle ___________ but they are! They live in ___________ (sometimes called troops). Each troop of gorillas is led by one ___________ male who likes nothing better than playing with his babies.

Gorillas are ___________ to look at. They are ___________ and have ___________ faces and big teeth. If any danger ___________ they beat their chests and roar to frighten away ___________ visitors. They may grow as tall as a man but often ___________ a lot more. They are too heavy to stay in the trees so they spend a lot of their time on the ground.

Gibbons live in the rain forests of Asia. They are very __________ apes. They can move very quickly __________ the trees, swinging and jumping among the __________. It often looks as __________ they are flying when they leap from tree to tree. They can leap as far as 15 metres! They have strong arms which are longer than their legs. Gibbons don't just swing through the trees. They also walk on their __________ legs and can run along very thin branches. Their coats are thick and __________, and keep out the __________ rain. Although they can look large and __________, they are very __________ and not really __________. Whenever there is any sign of an enemy they make loud hooting noises to frighten other animals away.

Test 4 The Big Race

After all the ____________, the day of the ____________ race had arrived at last. The competitors ____________ themselves with last minute preparations, tightening their laces and jumping up and down to ____________ up their muscles and relax the ____________. The rain came down in a steady drizzle but it did not manage to dampen the excitement everyone felt.

There was a moment of ____________ as the starter lined the ____________ up, followed by ____________ applause from the ____________ as the race started. Immediately a bunch of four of the best runners got out in ____________. Tim found himself just behind them. The ground got rough and ____________ as the children reached open ____________ and sped past fences and ____________.

Tim had practised hard for weeks and was really fit. He ran at a comfortable pace and soon began to catch up with the leaders. ____________ but surely he overtook three of them until only one runner was left in front of him.

Tim pounded away until there was only a short ____________ between them. Tim had an ____________ moment as he skidded on a muddy patch but ____________ he managed to keep his balance.

Ahead, Tim saw the finishing line. With one last ____________ effort he gritted his teeth and forced himself to run even faster. Almost at the last moment, Tim threw himself towards the line. Suddenly everyone was congratulating him. He could hardly ____________ it but ____________ he had somehow won.

Test 5 The Kangaroo

Kangaroos are one of the __________ animals alive. The modern kangaroo has evolved from ancestors __________ were in __________ thousands of years ago. Today we mostly find kangaroos in Australia. You can even find a kangaroo on the __________ coat of arms.

The kangaroo is a __________ (which means an animal with a pouch). When a baby kangaroo is born it has no fur and is only about three __________ long. The baby is completely __________ for __________ a long time. The female __________ her __________ in her pouch from __________ until they are a reasonable size and able to look after ___________. Even after a young kangaroo has been taught to walk by its mother, it likes to stay in the pouch to keep safe from enemies and ___________.

A fully grown kangaroo ___________ about two metres tall. It has short front legs with small paws and long powerful hind legs. These ___________ it to jump a distance of between three and five metres at a time! The kangaroo's long tail helps it to ___________ itself when jumping.

Kangaroos are hunted because they eat the farmers' crops and destroy the land. Kangaroo meat is used for food and its skin ___________ good leather. A kangaroo's ___________ is its speedy reactions, ___________ to move fast and its sharp hearing. Kangaroos use their powerful hind legs to kick with when ___________.

Test 6 The Olympic Games

The Olympic Games is an ___________ athletic competition, which takes place every four years. It is the modern ___________ of the Olympian Games. The Olympic Games first took place in the spring of 1896 and the Winter Olympics were first ___________ in 1924.

The Olympic Committee has the ___________ for ___________ the games. They ___________ where the games will take place. Athens was the site of the first Olympic Games. Athletes of all nations are ___________ to participate. They compete for one of three medals: bronze, silver and gold. All ___________ try to ___________ a gold medal.

Since the games began, ___________ by athletes have become ___________ better.

The Olympics ___________ open with an ___________ parade in which the athletes march into the stadium led by the Greek team, with the host nation marching in last. The Olympic Hymn is then played and the ___________ Olympic flag (five ___________ rings on a white ___________) is raised. An athlete then enters the stadium ___________ the Olympic torch which has been carried to the ___________ site by a relay of runners. The ___________ closes with the ___________ of doves, symbolizing the spirit of the games.

Test 7 Rivers of Fire

The ____________ of the Earth consists of hot, molten or ____________ rock and gas. Where the Earth's surface, or crust, is thin and weak these ____________ force their way through ____________ and form openings. These openings in the surface of the Earth are called ____________ . Some are simply long cracks in the ground. Other volcanoes look like cone-shaped ____________ with a hole at the top.

When the molten rock is inside the Earth, it is ____________ as magma. But as soon as it breaks out on to the Earth's surface, it is called lava. When the lava escapes from the volcano it covers the ____________ land. As lava flows, it cools and ____________. The ____________ lava piles up around the vent (the hole at the top of a volcano). ____________ and ash also pile up. These combine together to create the ____________ cone shape of the volcano.

A ____________ eruption is a ____________ sight to see. Hot lava bursts out of the volcano with an ____________ whooshing and roaring sound, ____________ sparks and ashes everywhere. Huge ____________ fountains of glowing lava leap high into the air and flow down the mountainside in ____________ red-hot rivers. These rivers of lava ____________ their way through anything that stands in their path. They may spread for miles and will ____________ everything they come into contact with.

Test 8 It's a Dog's Life

Katie loves dogs, but her cousin Mark is ___________ of them. ___________, he is always being ___________ by David, the son of Katie's new ___________. Every time David spots Mark walking down the road he lets his pet Alsatian into the garden just to ___________ Mark.

Katie decided to pay David a ___________ visit. When she knocked at the door his mother ___________. Katie said that she had promised to go for a walk with David and his dog that ___________. David's mother looked very pleased and ___________ that being new to the area he was finding it difficult to make new friends. David looked somewhat ___________.

A parents' guide to the spelling tests

Test 3

Gorillas and Gibbons

It is hard to believe that gorillas are really **shy**, gentle **animals** but they are! They live in **families** (sometimes called troops). Each troop of gorillas is led by one **powerful** male who likes nothing better than playing with his babies. Gorillas are **fearsome** to look at. They are **huge** and have **frightening** faces and big teeth. If any danger **threatens** they beat their chests and roar to frighten away **unwanted** visitors. They may grow as tall as a man but often **weigh** a lot more. They are too heavy to stay in the trees so they spend a lot of their time on the ground.

Gibbons live in the rain forests of Asia. They are very **acrobatic** apes. They can move very quickly **through** the trees, swinging and jumping among the **branches**. It often looks as **though** they are flying when they leap from tree to tree. They can leap as far as 15 metres! They have strong arms which are longer than their legs. Gibbons don't just swing through the trees. They also walk on their **hind** legs and can run along very thin branches. Their coats are thick and **woolly**, and keep out the **heaviest** rain. Although they can look large and **fierce**, they are very **friendly** and not really **dangerous**. Whenever there is any sign of an enemy they make loud hooting noises to frighten other animals away.

Test 4

The Big Race

After all the **waiting** the day of the **important** race had arrived at last. The competitors **busied** themselves with last minute preparations, tightening their laces and jumping up and down to **warm** up their muscles and relax the **tension**. The rain came down in a steady drizzle but it did not manage to dampen the excitement everyone felt.

There was a moment of **quietness** as the starter lined the **runners** up, followed by **enthusiastic** applause from the **crowd** as the race started. Immediately a bunch of four of the best runners got out in **front**. Tim found himself just behind them. The ground got rough and **uneven** as the children reached open **country** and sped past fences and **hedges**.

Tim had practised hard for weeks and was really fit. He ran at a comfortable pace and soon began to catch up with the leaders. **Slowly** but surely he overtook three of them until only one runner was left in front of him. Tim pounded away until there was only a short **distance** between them. Tim had an **anxious** moment as he skidded on a muddy patch but **luckily** he managed to keep his balance.

Ahead, Tim saw the finishing line. With one last **superhuman** effort he gritted his teeth and forced himself to run even faster. Almost at the last moment, Tim threw himself towards the line. Suddenly everyone was congratulating him. He could hardly **believe** it but **miraculously** he had somehow won.

Test 5

The Kangaroo

Kangaroos are one of the **strangest** animals alive. The modern kangaroo has evolved from ancestors **which** were in **existence** thousands of years ago. Today we mostly find kangaroos in Australia. You can even find a kangaroo on the **Australian** coat of arms.

The kangaroo is a **marsupial** (which means an animal with a pouch). When a baby kangaroo is born it has no fur and is only about three **centimetres** long. The baby is completely **helpless** for **quite** a long time. The female **carries** her **young** in her pouch from **birth** until they are a reasonable size and able to look after **themselves**. Even after a young kangaroo had been taught to walk by its mother it likes to stay in the pouch to keep safe from enemies and **predators**.

A fully grown kangaroo **measures** about two metres tall. It has short front legs with small paws and long powerful hind legs. These **enable** it to jump a distance of between three and five metres at a time! The kangaroo's long tail helps it to **balance** itself when jumping.

Kangaroos are hunted because they eat the farmers' crops and destroy the land. Kangaroo meat is used for food and its skin **produces** good leather. A kangaroo's **protection** is its speedy reactions, **ability** to move fast and its sharp hearing. Kangaroos use their powerful hind legs to kick with when **attacked**.

Test 6

The Olympic Games

The Olympic Games is an **international** athletic competition, which takes place every four years. It is the modern **revival** of the Olympian Games. The Olympic Games first took place in the spring of 1896 and the Winter Olympics were first **staged** in 1924.

The Olympic Committee has the **responsibility** for **planning** the games. They **decide** where the games will take place. Athens was the site of the first Olympic Games. Athletes of all nations are **eligible** to participate. They compete for one of three medals: bronze, silver and gold. All **competitors** try to **achieve** a gold medal.

Since the games began, **performances** by athletes have become **progressively** better.

The Olympics **traditionally** open with an **elaborate** parade in which the athletes march into the stadium, led by the Greek team, with the host nation marching in last. The Olympic Hymn is then played and the **official** Olympic flag (five **interlocking** rings on a white **background**) is raised. An athlete then enters the stadium **bearing** the Olympic torch which has been carried to the **present** site by a relay of runners. The **ceremony** closes with the **release** of doves, symbolizing the spirit of the games.

Test 7

Rivers of Fire

The **centre** of the Earth consists of hot, molten or **liquid** rock and gas. Where the Earth's surface, or crust, is thin and weak these **sometimes** force their way through **cracks** and form openings. These openings in the surface of the Earth are called **volcanoes**. Some are simply long cracks in the ground. Other volcanoes look like cone-shaped **mountains** with a hole at the top.

When the molten rock is inside the Earth, it is **known** as magma. But as soon as it breaks out on to the Earth's surface, it is called lava. When the lava escapes from the volcano it covers the **surrounding** land. As lava flows, it cools and **solidifies**. The **hardened** lava piles up around the vent (the hole at the top of a volcano). **Cinders** and ash also pile up. These combine together to create the **distinctive** cone shape of the volcano.

A **volcanic** eruption is a **spectacular** sight to see. Hot lava bursts out of the volcano with an **enormous** whooshing and roaring sound, **showering** sparks and ashes everywhere. Huge **fiery** fountains of glowing lava leap high into the air and flow down the mountainside in **deadly** red-hot rivers. These rivers of lava **scorch** their way through anything that stands in their path. They may spread for miles and will **destroy** everything they come into contact with.

Test 8

It's a Dog's Life

Katie loves dogs, but her cousin Mark is **terrified** of them. **Unfortunately**, he is always being **teased** by David, the son of Katie's new **neighbours**. Every time David spots Mark walking down the road he lets his pet Alsatian into the garden just to **scare** Mark.

Katie decided to pay David a **surprise** visit. When she knocked at the door his mother **answered**. Katie said that she had promised to go for a walk with David and his dog that **afternoon**. David's mother looked very pleased and **explained** that being new to the area he was finding it difficult to make new friends. David looked somewhat **embarrassed**.

Katie told David that he should **apologize** to Mark for frightening him and making his life a **misery**. After a lot of gentle **encouragement**, Katie **persuaded** Mark to meet David and his dog.

Mark was very **nervous** of the dog, but it sat quietly wagging its tail. Finally, Mark plucked up enough **courage** to stroke the dog's head.

Since then all three regularly meet to take the dog for a walk and **although** Mark is not **totally** at ease with the dog, his **confidence** is growing. Mark is right to be wary of dogs he doesn't know and is **sensible** to admire them from a distance at first.

Note: **apologize** may also be spelt **apologise**. Both answers are acceptable.

Test 9

Chef of the Year

Things were reaching boiling point in the **kitchen** as Simon prepared his meal for the judges in the Young Chef's competition. He had to prepare a two course meal on a budget of £12. Simon was ready for any **emergency**. In the fridge he had twice the **quantity** of **ingredients** just in case he needed a replacement if something went wrong.

While the young cooks were preparing their delicious dishes the judges wandered **casually** around the three **contestants** chatting about their concoctions.

In no time at all the lights started **flashing** and cooking time was up. The judges moved from table to table **tasting** the finalists' hard work whilst a camera crew searched for the best angles to film the **proceedings**.

The judges retired to **deliberate** and the **audience** were invited to taste the **luxury** food for themselves. The studio was full of squeals of **delight** as each dish was **savoured**.

Finally the **moment** of truth had arrived. The time all three had been waiting for with bated breath. Which finalist would be whisked off to a holiday **destination** wearing the crown of Young Chef of the Year?

The judges stepped forward to reveal their **verdict**. "Each cook has chosen a very **difficult** menu to prepare," said one, "and as always it has been very hard to arrive at a **decision**, but we are pleased to **announce** that Simon is this year's winner."

Test 10

Professor Inventalot Gets it Wrong

Professor Inventalot had been interested in **science** for as long as she **could** remember. When she had been a girl at **school**, she was always getting into trouble for **taking** things apart to see how they worked and not putting them back correctly. One day she dismantled her teacher's car but forgot to put the wheels back on! Now the professor was a **famous** inventor and gave **lectures** all over the world. However, she was still **forgetful** and still managed to make mistakes!

One day Professor Inventalot was working **hard** in her **laboratory**. On her door she put up a big notice saying DO NOT DISTURB. Scattered all over the floor were diagrams and plans. There were **switches** and **lights**, wires and tubes everywhere. A complicated arrangement of dials and weird-looking **instruments** were assembled and connected up on the **bench**. The professor was inventing her latest **incredible** machine.

Just as she was about to join the last two vital **pieces** together, the **telephone** rang and disturbed her concentration. Whilst she was talking, her pet poodle wandered in, decided that it was hungry and promptly ate the **instructions** that the professor had been working from! When the professor **returned** to complete the job, she **discovered** what had happened. Professor Inventalot sighed. "I **guess** I'll just have to try and remember what the next step was," she muttered – but this was the point at which everything started to go wrong!

Test 11

Schooling Without Schools

Imagine a book that **suddenly** comes to life, where the pages **actually** move and make sounds. With CD-ROMs this type of book has now **arrived**.

A CD-ROM is a disk used with a computer. When **loaded** into the computer, the computer screen displays words, **pictures**, sounds and **video**. (The **initials** CD-ROM stand for compact disk read only memory.)

CD-ROMs can store vast **amounts** of **information**, so a complete dictionary or encyclopaedia can be **stored** on one disk. Suppose you were doing a **project** on space – what better place to start your **research** than in an encyclopaedia on compact disk. You could read about **expeditions** to explore space, and look at photos of these adventures. There may be **recordings** of astronauts **talking** in space, and a video-clip of astronauts moving **carefully** in space. From the text **displayed** on the screen you could select the information you need.

Encyclopaedias on CD-ROMs are an **exciting** way of **finding** out about lots of **different** topics.

Key Stage 2

A parents' guide to the spelling tests

A parents' guide to the spelling tests

These parents' notes can be detached by carefully opening the wire staples, taking out the notes pages and then reclosing the staples.

This book enables your child to practise for the spelling test that forms part of the English National Tests at the end of Key Stage 2. This book contains 11 spelling tests.

As part of the English National Tests your child will also do a reading test and a writing test.

Most children at age 11 will be in the Level 3-5 range.

The spelling test at Key Stage 2 is primarily intended for children operating between Levels 3-5 of the National Curriculum. Children operating below these levels may find Key Stage 1 Spelling Tests useful.

About the spelling test

The spelling test at Key Stage 2 consists of a short passage containing missing words which the children are asked to spell. The passages in the book omit these words leaving spaces.

What is needed

For each test your child needs the workbook opened at the appropriate test and writing materials. You will need your copy of the notes for the test.

How to carry out a test

The test is designed so that it may be completed in one session. Each test should take in total about fifteen minutes.

Encourage your child to be relaxed and enjoy the test; it shouldn't be a source of tension for your child. Encourage your child to have a go at spelling words they are unfamiliar with. Allow sufficient time for each word to be written.

The practice sentences

Before doing a test for the first time, the practice sentences on the first page should be introduced to show your child what needs to be done. The practice sentences are shown below. Explain that there are some words missing from the sentences. Ask your child to follow the sentences as you read the passage aloud to them, but not to write anything yet.

Practice sentences:

What a lovely surprise! What **fun** they would have! John stood and **looked** at the poster **with** excitement. The **fair** was coming to town. He rushed around to tell his friends the **good** news.

Now read the passage again, telling your child the missing word and giving your child time to write the missing words in. Go through the passage afterwards to make sure your child has got the idea.

A parents' guide to the spelling tests

The spelling tests

Each time you do a spelling test use these instructions:

1 I am going to read a passage called ______ (title of passage). Find this in your book. The passage in your book has some words missing. Listen carefully and follow the story in your book. Don't write anything yet. (Now read the passage to them. The passages are printed at the end of these parents' notes.)

2 I am going to read the passage again. When you come to a gap, wait for me to tell you the word and then write it in the space. If you are not sure how to spell the word have a go and write the letters you think look right.

3 Read the rest of the passage through, pausing at each missing word.

Marking the tests

1 For each correct spelling give one mark. Add up the marks and write the totals on the table on page 32.

2 To find the National Curriculum level use the table below. Look at the total marks and see which level these marks correspond to, for example, a score between 1 and 3 equals level 2. (NB This table is only a guide; a child's level will be determined by their overall performance in the English tests.)

Score	*Level 2*	*Level 3*	*Level 4*	*Level 5*	*Level 6*
1-3	*				
3-6		*			
7-13			*		
14-18				*	
19-20					*

Analysing spelling errors

The errors children make may be used as a basis for further spelling practice. Sometimes the errors may be clustered together as a general difficulty. Some of the most common at this stage are:

1 relying too much on the phonic analysis of words (the way words sound)

2 problems with prefixes at the beginning of words, e.g. as in disappear, or suffixes at the end of words, e.g. as in helpful

3 a lack of awareness of basic spelling rules, e.g. drop the e before adding ing as in baking

4 an inability to break words up into smaller parts, i.e. syllables.

The **WH Smith Spelling Lists** series provides reinforcement of key spelling rules and useful spelling practice.

Complete Story Texts

Test 1

Camping Capers

"That spot looks **ideal** for camping," shouted Jane, pointing to a clearing in the **field**.

"Great," **replied** Paul, "but let's camp closer to the stream, it'll be handy for washing up and **rinsing** our clothes." Paul was always looking for the easy **option**.

Having **pitched** the tent they searched through the **equipment** to find the camping stove and set about cooking their first meal under the stars. It tasted **delicious**.

"What a life!" sighed Paul. "Away from the hustle and bustle of the city with nothing but blue **skies**, trees and green, green grass as far as the eye can see."

"Don't forget the cows **grazing** in the field," said Jane. They sat talking for ages before **finally** climbing into their sleeping bags and **settling** down for the night.

Just as dawn broke they were **rudely** awoken by the sound of **hooves**. "What's going on?" asked Paul **sleepily**.

Before Jane could answer, a loud mooing noise was heard and then a cow's head **appeared** through the tent flaps.

"We're surrounded by cows!" exclaimed Paul. He **watched** in **amazement** as the herd marched past the tent and began to drink from the stream. "Oh no, that stream must be their **regular** drinking place!" he groaned.

"So much for the countryside being **peaceful**," teased Jane.

Test 2

Lost!

The journey up the mountain road was exciting as the car wound its **way** around hairpin bends with **steep** rocky cliffs on either **side**. Amtiaz and Shirin looked out of the window breathlessly as the car **climbed** slowly upwards with its **engine** straining.

Soon their father turned off the main road on to a narrow mountain track, leading into a wooded **valley**, filled with pine trees. They found a clearing near a stream, where the water gurgled and bubbled happily along. It was a **beautiful** place to stop. Amtiaz and Shirin jumped **quickly** out of the car and raced to **explore** the area whilst their parents were busy laying out a blanket on the ground and getting out the picnic things.

The children threw rocks into the stream to make **stepping** stones. Amtiaz roared with **laughter** as Shirin slipped and **splashed** into the water as they crossed to the other side. The adults were still preparing the picnic so the children **decided** to follow the narrow path into the forest.

Deeper and deeper it took them until they were **wrapped** in the **stillness** of the forest and could no longer hear the **voices** of their parents. **Although** it was getting a little creepy, the children dared each other to continue until the path seemed to **disappear** altogether. As they looked back **everything** looked different. **Suddenly** they realized they were lost.

Katie told David that he should __________ to Mark for frightening him and making his life a __________. After a lot of gentle __________, Katie __________ Mark to meet David and his dog.

Mark was very __________ of the dog, but it sat quietly wagging its tail. Finally, Mark plucked up enough __________ to stroke the dog's head.

Since then all three regularly meet to take the dog for a walk and __________ Mark is not __________ at ease with the dog, his __________ is growing. Mark is right to be wary of dogs he doesn't know and is __________ to admire them from a distance at first.

Test 9 Chef of the Year

Things were reaching boiling point in the __________ as Simon prepared his meal for the judges in the Young Chef's competition. He had to prepare a two course meal on a budget of £12. Simon was ready for any __________. In the fridge he had twice the __________ of __________ just in case he needed a replacement if something went wrong.

While the young cooks were preparing their delicious dishes, the judges wandered __________ around the three __________ chatting about their concoctions.

In no time at all the lights started __________ and cooking time was up. The judges moved from table to table __________ the finalists' hard work whilst a camera crew searched for the best angles to film the __________.

The judges retired to __________ and the __________ were invited to taste the __________ food for themselves. The studio was full of squeals of ____________ as each dish was ____________.

Finally the ____________ of truth had arrived. The time all three had been waiting for with bated breath. Which finalist would be whisked off to a holiday ____________ wearing the crown of Young Chef of the Year?

____

The judges stepped forward to reveal their ____________. "Each cook has chosen a very ____________ menu to prepare," said one, "and as always it has been very hard to arrive at a ____________, but we are pleased to ____________ that Simon is this year's winner."

Test 10 Professor Inventalot Gets it Wrong!

Professor Inventalot had been interested in ___________ for as long as she ___________ remember. When she had been a girl at ___________, she was always getting into trouble for ___________ things apart to see how they worked and not putting them back correctly. One day she dismantled her teacher's car but forgot to put the wheels back on! Now the professor was a ___________ inventor and gave ___________ all over the world. However, she was still ___________ and still managed to make mistakes!

One day Professor Inventalot was working ___________ in her ___________. On her door she put up a big notice saying DO NOT DISTURB. Scattered all over the floor were diagrams and plans. There were ___________ and ___________, wires and tubes everywhere. A complicated arrangement of dials and weird-looking ___________ were assembled and connected up on the ___________. The professor was inventing her latest ___________ machine.

Just as she was about to join the last two vital ____________ together, the ____________ rang and disturbed her concentration. Whilst she was talking, her pet poodle wandered in, decided that it was hungry and promptly ate the ____________ that the professor had been working from! When the professor ____________ to complete the job, she ____________ what had happened. Professor Inventalot sighed. "I ____________ I'll just have to try and remember what the next step was," she muttered – but this was the point at which everything started to go wrong!

Test II Schooling Without Schools

Imagine a book that ___________ comes to life, where the pages ___________ move and make sounds. With CD-ROMs this type of book has now ___________.

A CD-ROM is a disk used with a computer. When ___________ into the computer, the computer screen displays words, ___________, sounds and ___________. (The ___________ CD ROM stand for compact disk read only memory.)

CD-Roms can store vast ___________ of ___________,
so a complete dictionary or encyclopaedia can be
___________ on one disk. Suppose you were doing a
___________ on space – what better place to start your
___________ than in an encyclopaedia on compact disk.
You could read about ___________ to explore space,
and look at photos of these adventures. There may be
___________ of astronauts ___________ in space, and a
video-clip of astronauts moving ___________ in space.
From the text ___________ on the screen you could
select the information you need.

Encyclopaedias on CD-Roms are an ___________ way of
___________ out about lots of ___________ topics.

Test	Date	Score
Camping Capers		
Lost!		
Gorillas and Gibbons		
The Big Race		
The Kangaroo		
The Olympic Games		
Rivers of Fire		
It's a Dog's Life		
Chef of the Year		
Professor Inventalot Gets it Wrong		
Schooling Without Schools		